OPEN QUESTIONS IN WORSHIP

Gordon Lathrop, Series Editor

What is "contemporary" worship?

Paul Westermeyer

Paul Bosch

Marianne Sawicki

D1279610

Augsburg Fortress
PUBLISHERS

Minneapolis

OPEN QUESTIONS IN WORSHIP
What is "contemporary" worship?

ISBN 0-8066-2798-0
ISSN 1080-0565

Scripture quotations, unless otherwise noted, are from the New Revised Standard Version Bible © 1989 Division of Christian Education of the National Council of the Churches of Christ in the United States of America. Used by permission.

Cover and interior design: Ann Elliot Artz
Cover photo: Ann Elliot Artz

Manufactured in the U.S.A.   10-27980

| 00 | 99 | 98 | 97 | 96 | 95 | 1 | 2 | 3 | 4 | 5 | 6 | 7 | 8 | 9 | 0 |

CONTENTS

FOREWORD

One of the most pressing of current questions in worship is, How can our worship be contemporary? And when that question has been asked, the questions of *music* and of *multiple services* are not far behind: What music shall we use? Should we plan a different kind of music than we are using now? Should we schedule more than one kind of service, a "menu" of liturgies? Is it a good idea to call one service "traditional" and one service "contemporary"? Under these questions, there lurks a yet more reflective, more troubling one: What do we mean by "contemporary" anyway?

These are not abstract questions. They are arising with urgency in many parishes and worshiping communities today, and they seem to ask for immediate response.

This book comes with these very questions in mind. It seeks to give practical, concrete help. But it asks you to slow down a little, to think about the issues. It proposes that you might want to come to a lively answer to these questions in a way that is peaceful and faithful, not anxious and fear-driven.

Granted that we all agree that our assemblies must be marked by the essentials of Christian worship, these are *open* questions. That is, worship is made up of a participating assembly gathered around scripture read and preached, baptism celebrated or remembered, the holy supper held, and these things done so that the gospel of Jesus Christ might be shown forth in clarity. From agreement on these essentials we can go on to discuss freely the nature of our music, the details of our schedule, and the quality of our relationship to the current culture. When, however, these questions of "contemporaneity" push the essentials—the *center*—out of the way, they are no longer open, no longer places for legitimate discussion and difference, trial and error, sorting and success. Rather, they become marks of our own infidelity.

The authors in the current volume are committed to what is essential

4

in Christian worship. They also are engaged in proposing their own answers to the open questions. Paul Westermeyer thinks that there always should be *at least two kinds of music.* Paul Bosch proposes that there should be *only one service.* Marianne Sawicki thinks that worship should be neither "contemporary" nor "traditional." Or maybe it should be both. In any case, it should be *time therapy* for all of us who are "time victims." These are clear and vigorous proposals. They call for your thought, perhaps your disagreement—but, in any case, your engagement in the open questions.

How do you answer their proposals?

Rejoice with the writers in the gifts of God that are at the center of Christian worship, and be welcome to the open questions.

Gordon Lathrop
General Editor

What music should we use in worship?

Paul Westermeyer

I f the practice of most of the church for the last twenty centuries and the seventh article of the Augsburg Confession are correct, word and sacrament constitute the center of Christian worship. On the Lord's Day of resurrection, therefore, baptized Christians have characteristically gathered to hear the word of God, to intercede for the world, to take a collection for the poor, and to bring gifts of bread and wine that are then received as bearers of the grace of God in Christ. Around that central Sunday service of Holy Communion, Christians have also developed services for daily prayer. These have taken any number of forms: the prayers of individuals or of families in the morning, at evening, and at meals; the prayer life of monastic communities that have extended these "hours" or "offices" of prayer throughout the day and night; the public prayer of schools or churches or ecumenical gatherings of Christians.

The psalms, New Testament canticles, and the church's hymns have served as central vehicles for Christians to express their praise and prayer with all its lament, anger, joy, grief, and gratitude. If the practice of most of the church and especially of the Lutheran tradition is any indication, there is delight in singing as many of these and other texts as possible. Given that eagerness to sing, a group of worshipers is immediately confronted with the question, What music should we use?

There are two extreme ways to answer this question. One is to try to fashion a musical language that is as esoteric as possible in an attempt to make the musical style distinct from that of the surrounding culture. The other answer is to try to embrace the sounds of the surrounding culture so as to avoid any musical distinctions with it.

These two extremes are theoretical possibilities that are difficult, if not impossible, to achieve in practice. For example, even when the Shakers sought to create their own unique sounds with their own particular notation, they still were influenced by musical materials from the United States and the British Isles. It is impossible to avoid the surrounding musical culture altogether. The most a community can do is to attempt to restrict itself to a certain past, and even that is very difficult; it requires being walled off from the world.

On the other hand, a community that attempts self-consciously to use the culture's sounds inevitably will fashion its own distinctive communal "bank" of sounds and rhythms. The longer any community exists, the more its musical life will take on characteristics that are separate from the surrounding culture. That is simply a reflection of the inescapable reality that any group that sings or makes music together over time will create its own musical life, its own tradition. Visiting virtually any ongoing worshiping community reveals that immediately.

These two extreme theoretical answers to the question of what music to use are matched by the very practical influences of the broader and smaller communities in which we live. We exist in a world of rhythm and sound that comes from both the larger culture around us and the smaller culture of our specific worshiping community. These two penetrate one another, but they also have lives of their own. It is virtually impossible to escape either. The community that adopts the world's sounds moves toward its own uniqueness in spite of itself. Even a hermit has an inner communal memory.

Initial considerations

Living in these communities of sound requires the church to make choices. Ongoing communities of worship inherit a certain music, and in some times and places little if any choice seems necessary. At other times—like ours—when there are so many possibilities and so many opinions about those possibilities, the church is forced to make choices. If it attempts to be faithful, it will make these choices consciously and intentionally. Then considerations like the following are called into play.

1. *What associations does the music have?* The early church chose to reject instrumental music because of its associations, for them, with immorality and idolatry. The church in the West has chosen to re-think that decision and no longer views instrumental music as having such associations, so that at the end of the twentieth century, instrumental music as a whole is not problematic for most churches. The question concerns more generally what kind of music churches should use. A "jazz mass" illustrates how that question can receive different answers. For some people jazz calls to mind the prostitution district of New Orleans or Guy Lombardo and New Years' Eve. For others it reflects the most creative and "spiritual" energies of our period.

There is no eternal equation here that says a certain style is by definition good or bad. At different times and places, as for different people in those times and places, certain kinds of music will have different associations.

To make sense of the associations and to decide what will and will not be used requires historical understanding and considerable pastoral concern.

2. Though there are different associations that may vary from place to place and time to time, there are also basic theological presuppositions that are not tied to a given time and place. One of these calls rhythm and sound into play.

Rhythm relates to the body. When nearly arrhythmic, music can suggest a sort of motionless contemplation that transcends or denies the physicality of our being. At its pulsating extreme, music leads to a celebrative and even frenzied dance that affirms or celebrates the physicality of our being. Likewise, *sound relates to the body.* It can move from the ethereal out-of-body sound of the unchanged child's voice to the rich bodily and sexual sound of the changed male or female voice.

There are motifs in the Christian message that suggest both of these possibilities. Jesus prepared for his ministry in the wilderness, came apart from the crowds and prayed, and in many respects transcended or even denied the physical reality of the bodily world. Christ also cared for the sick, however, and was concerned about the physical being of people. Christians affirm that in Christ, God took flesh among us and thereby forcefully affirmed and even celebrated the physical.

Christian communities have tended to gravitate to one or the other of these tendencies. The contemplative possibilities are suggested by some models of Gregorian chant, by transcendent interpretations of Renaissance polyphony, or by boy choirs. The more bodily affirmations are suggested by some Spanish masses that feel like fiestas, by the bold pulsations of sixteenth century rhythmic chorales, or by the richest possible vocal sounds human beings can make.

Theologians and communities have to sort this out for themselves, but at either extreme there can be trouble. All contemplation can deny the incarnation, lead to passivism, and avoid the world Christians are called to serve. All bodily celebration can deny the silence of prayer, the necessity for retreating into the wilderness, and turn into a self-centered orgy. The church at its healthiest holds these two realities in tension and in actual musical practice lives out the paradoxical wholeness of the Christian message.

3. *The incarnation has led the church to sing its faith in the musical language of the people who embrace its message.* That is, the message takes musical shape not in the abstract, but in the actual "incarnate" ethnic sounds of given peoples. English, French, African, Spanish, German, Swedish, Welsh, Chinese, and all other peoples of the globe sing it in their native tongues and in the musical contours that accompany those tongues. Today's multicultural concerns are simply the continuation of what the church has been doing for twenty centuries—figuring out how to allow the message

of the gospel to take form in sound among people all over the world, whatever their language and music may be.

There is an opposing consideration, however. The incarnational reality of the gospel also means that it ties specific times, places, and peoples together. The gospel is not only incarnational in the sense that it is particular. It is also incarnational in the sense that it is for all peoples and makes of us one body in Christ. If that is true, *there must be some way in which we not only sing our individual ethnic songs, but also sing something more universal.*

This universal or catholic reality will always be a broken one in a world that is itself broken. But we are made one body in Christ nonetheless. This one body has entered our actual history. The victory of Christ over sin and death is not only above history; it is also realized among us, the one body of Christ. That needs to take concrete musical expression somehow. This is not only a theological affirmation; it is a pastoral necessity. People who move from place to place, which in our nomadic culture has become virtually normative, need to be able to sing with their sisters and brothers in Christ.

This means that again two realities need to be worked out in tension. One is the particular ethnic music in which the gospel is sung. The other is the universal song of one body that ties together the particularity of our individual ethnic identities. One way to keep these two realities in tension is to sing both our own songs and those of others. That affirms the grace of God among us and our relationship with other Christians. It indicates that alone we are incomplete and need the music of other Christians to complement ours.

4. We are not only in communion with Christians around the world who live now. *We are in communion with our sisters and brothers in Christ who have preceded us.* They have left us an amazingly rich legacy of music. If we are wise, we will utilize this huge repertoire not only because it keeps us connected with them, but also because much of the music that remains to us from them has been tested and found worth our while. History is the best judge of what is worth keeping, and we do well to heed its lessons.

Once again two truths are held in tension, this time the old and the new. If we are faithful, we will sing both old and new music.

Actually this old and new music is one single new song, because newness is not identifiable with a literally "new" song, which after one singing becomes old anyway. The new song refers to what happens over and over again to the literally "old" and to the literally "new": Qualitatively new resurrection life is breathed into our oldness, which is composed of both the literally old and the literally new.

5. This suggests another central consideration, namely, that *the church is in but not of the world.* The church uses the physical stuff of the world,

including God's gift of music, in all its old and new forms. All the old and new stuff of the creation, including music, is broken by the reality of what Christians call sin, but we are still called to use it. God does not come to us unmediated, but through the physical stuff of the good but broken creation—like words, water, bread, and wine. Human beings in their cultural settings fashion the broken gift of music into artistic forms. These are used in worshiping assemblies and there are broken anew to the new life of the gospel.

That is, the message of the gospel comes in the medium of music, of old clay pots, old broken vessels, even when it appears to be new. The message is never identifiable with the broken medium, but the medium is nonetheless the bearer of the message. The church is in but not of the world in its music as well as in everything else. Its music, like everything else, is refashioned by God in Christ through the Holy Spirit to qualitatively new life.

A more central matter

To ask about old and new music is important, but it evades a more central question. That question has to do with what music fits our worship. It is really not a question of old or new, or of musical style at all, but a question rather of genre, of form, of what music "works" and makes sense in Christian worship. This question stimulates another set of considerations.

One of the central features of Christian worship is that it *points beyond itself to what God does.* Indeed, Christian worship, like the Christian gospel that it expresses, turns everything upside down: It looks like what we do, but in fact God graces us—comes to us in word and sacrament. It turns out that God is the actor, and we are the recipients of God's gracious acting.

That means worship is qualitatively different from all other public gatherings of people. Those who lead worship and the whole body of worshipers as well are called not to point to themselves as entertainers do, but to point beyond themselves to the God who transcends and transforms them.

Music has to do the same thing. Its role in worship is not to call attention to itself, but to point beyond itself to the God who created it in the first place.

This can be taken to mean using a single very restricted musical style or a few very restricted musical styles. Restricting musical styles would be a mistake because it disregards the human crafting of the raw materials of God's good gift of music, and none of that crafting and experience should be written out of worship. Music that is quiet, loud, motionless, pulsating, old, new, more or less popular all has a place in our worship. What pointing beyond itself means is that the context of worship needs to control what we do musically so that music fits the flow and the essential actions of worship, rather than our own purposes.

This suggests that the real issue is that the liturgy—by which I mean the deep structures of word and sacrament, and not the more superficial matters of ceremony or style—needs to be respected so that our own egos can be hidden, that music may point beyond itself to the God who gave it to us in the first place. This means that virtually any kind of music can be used, as long as it makes sense in the flow of the liturgy. One aims, of course, for the best possible music, because worship is the most important thing human beings do, because people need to be treated with respect, and because worship continues over time and needs music that is as durable as possible. But even "bad" music can be used in the liturgy and make some sense because the liturgy has the capacity to contextualize everything. The liturgy can make even poor quality rise above itself and eventually lead of necessity to the finest quality. This is not an argument for poor quality. It is an argument for keeping our priorities straight, and this suggests several things.

Music of the congregation needs to be congregational. Old or new or specific styles are not nearly so important as whether unrehearsed congregations can sing the music. Congregations cannot count irregular or lengthy rests from any period or style. They cannot do overly complicated syncopations. They cannot, as a rule, sing augmented fourths or major sevenths or other such leaps that are not carefully prepared. They cannot generally sing what is conceived for a soloist. They cannot sing music that avoids a tonal or modal center or meanders without musical coherence.

Congregations can sing refrains. They can sing the coherent strophic musical structures of hymn tunes. They can sing psalm tones. They can sing what moves around a tonal or modal center in the manner of folk music. What they sing may be in any number of styles, old or new— Gregorian chant, sixteenth-century German chorale tunes, Genevan psalm tunes, African American spirituals, white spirituals, nineteenth-century hymn tunes, twentieth-century psalm tones, materials from Taizé, percussive African music, and so forth. What is important here is not style, but what people can sing. The worshiping assembly can do what human beings without rehearsal can do—sing simple musical structures in an idiom they understand, structures that make logical musical sense, so that they can be remembered easily enough for singing among normal people.

Of course, this requires teaching and has to bear some relation to a musical language that is in the ear of the people. Unless a group chooses to be a sect and shuts itself off entirely from the world so that it retains in its ear a musical language that is distinct from the culture, this will mean some sort of relation to the broader culture's musical language. But the culture's music always needs to be viewed critically. This is true partly because the church has a history of sound that should be respected and

utilized, partly because of the danger of thoughtlessly embracing associations that the church does not want to embrace, but also because not
everything in the culture will work. Trying to adapt what is soloistic or
filled with rests or overly complex syncopations to a community of worshipers leads to frustration and ultimately silence from the worshipers.
This does not mean worshipers cannot be challenged. It simply means
their particular medium has to be respected.

Their particular medium has two further characteristics that we sometimes seem prone to forget. First, it is acoustic, that is, it is made by human
beings with their natural human voices. Amplified sound used for leading,
because it is unnatural, tends to discourage rather than encourage communal singing. Second, it is live, that is, it is made by real human beings
in a particular time and place. Using what is pre-recorded as a substitute
for the congregation removes the central sound of worship itself—the
congregation's sound. Using pre-recorded sounds also discourages congregational singing because it cannot respond to real people in their unique
place who are tired or lively, sick or well, who have just experienced
certain joys and sorrows. All of these matters require the sensitivity of live
musical leadership.

*A group of voices we call a choir can do all sorts of things a congre-
gation cannot do, because it rehearses.* It rehearses on behalf of the
congregation and must begin with congregational song because its fundamental role is to lead the congregation. Beyond that, however, there is
no limit to what a choir can do as long as the requirements of the liturgy—
which includes the pastoral needs of the people and the ethical demands
of the moment—are respected.

This means it can alternate with the congregation on stanzas of hymns,
using the simplest and most complex music, old or new. It can do psalm
settings, anthems, proper verses, and offertories from many periods and
styles. It can sing before and after a service. All of this is possible with
the wide repertoire of music the church has produced for choirs, as long
as it does not overwhelm the liturgy or displace the primary voice of
congregational singing. Festive occasions can sometimes exceed the normal boundaries of time, but even then a sense of proper proportion is
required. While music before or after a service can be longer and festive
occasions can modify the norm, an anthem or a Sanctus that turns the
liturgy into a choral performance and dwarfs everything else destroys the
balance and essence of worship.

*Organists, single instrumentalists, and instrumental ensembles are
essentially extensions of the choir.* They can do all the things the choir
can do, except sing words (and, if they sing, they can do that also). They
are especially able to accompany actions; provide intonations, introduc-
tions, interludes, and harmonizations before and during sung portions of
the service; and can also respond in quiet or jubilant meditation or praise.

Bands, orchestras, and other instrumental ensembles, especially wind ensembles (which make sound the way the human voice does with breath), work well as long as they and their directors understand the nature of worship. Groups cannot respond to the moment the way a single player can, however, and it is difficult and prohibitively expensive to assemble instrumental ensembles for rehearsals and services week after week. This is why organs have come to be associated with Christian worship. They put a remarkable and fitting wind ensemble of sound that fills large spaces under the control of a single player who can respond to the moment more easily than a group, and who (for good or ill) costs less and can schedule practice times more easily than groups.

Musicians all need to operate under the same discipline as other leaders in worship. They, more than any others, have the capacity to overwhelm a congregation with sound or to ignore their leadership roles altogether. In either case, they call undue attention to themselves and not only confuse a worshiping congregation, but change it into something that contradicts its very nature.

Challenges we face

At the moment we live in a culture in which music is used to sell things. Whole industries work at marketing, and music is one of their chief tools. Jingles and mood music accompany us everywhere—on the radio, on television, in movies, at shopping malls, in elevators, on telephones, in our automobiles. It should not surprise us that the church has been influenced by these currents and has seen in them new opportunities for evangelism.

There is a well-meaning intent here, but one must ask if an unfortunate sleeper does not lurk within it. If worship turns into a sales pitch in which music becomes the commercial jingle, it is easy to view music as culprit or solution to all our problems. But does not such a view both oversimplify and avoid the central issue? Isn't the fundamental consideration this: If it is possible to market the Christian gospel the way one markets other products, then is God necessary at all? Is the grace of God necessary or simply irrelevant?

The issue here would seem not to be musical at all, but to be deeply theological with the most practical of ethical implications and consequences. It relates fundamentally to the grace of God and the gospel's power to free us from trying to manipulate or control one another, even when done with the best of intentions.

The reason this impinges on music is because music is one of God's gifts that so easily can be misused to control people. A large part of the church musician's vocation is to care for the gift of music responsibly. To use it with manipulative intent is a serious ethical lapse.

This means making judgments about what music is used and how it is used. The church as a whole will do this over time. The church musician's vocation is to do this for the local assembly, so that congregations in their worship do not waste their time on what is not worth their while or become ensnared by what is misused.

Musicians need to make judgments with a great deal of humility and pastoral care. They may make mistakes because they are human. Their task is a difficult one, but to evade it is to evade part of their vocation and responsibility to the people they are called to serve. What protects the musician and the rest of the church from being manipulated is the quality of the music that is chosen, how it is used, and the liturgy itself.

This brings us back to where we began, to the context of music in the church and to the two extreme options: either a wholesale rejection of the music of the surrounding culture or a wholesale embrace of it. The first of these attempts presumes a sect that walls itself off from the world. The second turns the church into a reflection of the dominant characteristics of the culture in which it exists.

Christian communities have to sort this out for themselves. I would suggest that neither response is adequate for the church. The church can respect and use its past music and the distance from the contemporary world that past music creates. It will also use the music of the present as it lives within a particular culture. It will use music that normal people can sing without rehearsal and music that requires rehearsing by a trained group.

Mostly, it will turn to the psalms and express the height and depth of their praise, prayer, laments, gratitude, joy, grief, and sorrow, which they express so eloquently against the backdrop of God's grace. And it will do so with the richly varied music these themes suggest.

ABOUT THE AUTHOR

Paul Westermeyer is Professor of Church Music at Luther Seminary in St. Paul, Minnesota.

Shall we schedule a menu of worship services?

Paul Bosch

S hould a parish schedule two services, one "contemporary" and one "traditional"? My answer is, No. In this essay I will present my reasons for this answer. But let me speak as forcefully as possible. As the philosopher once observed, in some contexts it is more important that a proposition be interesting than that it be true. In the passionate exchange of opinion, guided by the Spirit, the truth will emerge (see Acts 5:38-39). Let me be provocative in my statement of the case, so that no one fails to understand the point.

My own conclusions—still more or less tentative, I confess, but increasingly persuasive to me—include a suspicion that multiple Sunday services exact a terrible price in contemporary church life, they are unfaithful ecclesiologically, and they are inimical to the needs of contemporary worship.

The proliferation of worship services in North America can be dated to those heady days of optimism and plenty just after World War II, when church membership rolls were burgeoning and new church buildings were springing up in every suburban subdivision. It seemed then—I was myself a young pastor—that multiple Sunday services were a logical and self-evident elaboration in the advancement of God's dominion.

One hears these days, however, of congregations offering multiple services in bewildering combination and variety. Some congregations offer three or four identical traditional services each weekend. Other congregations offer each Sunday both a traditional service and a contemporary service. Still others offer both a "believers' service" and a "seekers' service"; or a traditional service and a "youth service"; or a "quiet, contemplative service," by which is often meant a simple service with much silence and with little or no music. One hears of congregations offering in their many worship "opportunities" a "Country and Western service."

I have come to believe that the principle of "one flock, one shepherd" (John 10:16) ought to be normative among us. "One flock, one shepherd" is not just a christological confession; it is an ecclesial confession as well.

Let me identify at least four reasons to be suspicious of the movement to proliferate Sunday worship "opportunities," as they are sometimes advertised. They are the pastoral-professional, the sociological, the theological-ecclesial, and the liturgical.

The *pastoral-professional* reason is simple: multiple Sunday services deplete the pastor's energies, often unnecessarily. There are unimaginable demands placed upon faithful parish pastors these days; multiple Sunday services need not add to their burden. When we ask an individual pastor to preside and preach at more than one Sunday service ("two flocks, one shepherd"), we are in effect turning that pastor into a nineteenth-century circuit-rider.

Perhaps more persuasive is the second reason to be wary of multiple Sunday services: the *sociological.* To introduce a second Sunday service in a single parish ("two flocks, one shepherd") is to divide the congregation unnecessarily. Those who come to the nine o'clock service soon do not know those who attend the eleven o'clock service. We have in effect produced two distinct parishes, each with its own sociological characteristics. For instance, the young families may come at nine, and the elderly at eleven. In my view, that is not a wholesome picture of the catholicity of the church.

Young families need to see and know the elderly, and vice versa; "believers" need to see and know the "seekers," and vice versa; "traditionalists" need to see and know the "contemporary" crowd (however they may be defined), and vice versa. In fact, one of the chief glories of Christian worship, in our already tragically divided and segregated North American society, has been the compelling witness to our unity-in-diversity at the table of the Lord: rich and poor, old and young, black and white, gay and straight, political left and political right.

If we lose this welcome diversity in any of our worshiping assemblies, if we begin to "market" worship to specific sociological segments of the total human population, then we have lost something incalculably precious. We have sold out to consumerism.

That leads to the *theological-ecclesial* argument. To offer within a single parish distinct "worship opportunities," in a variety of time periods and a variety of styles, is to deny the catholicity—the splendid, rich, and even contradictory fullness—of the church and to obscure such catholicity among the people of God.

Let us consider this: Such a diverse congregation will rarely "grow" as some would like to see "growth." *It may be that only those congregations will "grow" that are fully homogeneous: all of one color, all of one age, all of one opinion, all of one sociological or economic class.* Indeed, even in "one flock, one shepherd" parishes, each assembly of worshipers, over time, takes on its own distinctive personality.

But is numerical growth an inherent good? Could it be that some growth is achieved at too high a cost: at the expense of faithfulness to the gospel and its welcome of diversity? Jesus, after all, did not urge "success" on his followers; he urged faithfulness. "The gate is wide and the road is easy that leads to destruction ... [but] the gate is narrow and the road is hard that leads to life" (Matthew 7:13-14).

Finally, there is the *liturgical* argument. Multiple services encourage a perception in Christian communities that worship consists of laypeople coming to their ordained clergy to be "filled," as to a gas station—an ancient misperception with a contemporary twist. Such misperceptions effectively deny not only our oneness in Christ, but also our understanding of worship as the work of the people. Have we succumbed to our era's demonic addiction to consumerism? Have our clergy become purveyors of "designer liturgies"—a liturgy for every taste and preference?

Do we really want our Christian congregations to be perceived as the local "religion franchise"? That is precisely the liturgical temptation with multiple services: to succumb to an entrepreneurial, market-driven vision of the Christian mission. This vision allows congregations at worship to become religious consumers: patronized by laypeople, but "owned and operated" by ordained clergy who must dream up ever more clever menus and premiums, ever more ingenious marketing promotions to keep the customers coming in the door.

One hears this question: What if it becomes a matter of space? What if the entire worshiping membership of a congregation cannot fit into the congregation's building at the same time? Then that is another matter altogether. I suppose multiple Sunday services then become a necessity, if one is unwilling to begin another congregation. But multiple services should be understood as an unfortunate necessity. The price to be paid is still enormous, and that price will be exacted, inevitably and inexorably. "One flock, one shepherd" as an ecclesial principle cries out, in my view, for vigorous investigation.

What of congregations, for instance, with multiple services and multiple ordained clergy on their staff ("Two flocks, two shepherds")? And—for that matter—what of multiple Christian congregations in a single city? Is the proliferation of distinct and separate congregations in a given geographical area somehow a necessary but lamentable compromise with the "one flock, one shepherd" principle? One wonders how the church at Ephesus struggled with that issue when the number of worshipers became too large to meet in the same house church. There are questions of ecclesiology here that remain largely unaddressed.

What I am proposing is nothing less than an invitation to a radical rethinking of ecclesiology, with some almost frightening consequences.

Is there an optimum size for the membership of a Christian congregation? I would say, Yes. Years ago one of my favorite theologians suggested that the rediscovery of the cellular nature of the church is the most exciting ecumenical development of the twentieth century. What we know as "the church" is actually a living organism, composed of many different layers of cells and tissues and members, each with its own function and each, perhaps, with its own optimum size. The structure that we have come to know as the contemporary Christian congregation represents, after all, only one level in that taxonomy.

Is there an optimum size for a Christian church building? I say, Yes. One of my colleagues has this rule of thumb: If the church building needs a public address system, it's too big.

Lest I be misunderstood, I want to make clear my respect for the positive contributions to contemporary church life from the so-called church growth movement and its liturgical manifestation, the so-called entertainment evangelism movement. They have much to teach the church: an infectious enthusiasm in worship leaders; a burning desire to be hospitable and welcoming to all; an energetic and effective program of follow-up for visitors and the assimilation of new members. Would that all Christian congregations possessed these splendid gifts of the Spirit!

And—lest I be misunderstood—my argument here applies equally to traditional multiple services. The question, as I have come to perceive it, is not "traditional" versus "contemporary." It is not "believers" versus "seekers." The question is deeper: I am proposing an alternate and, I believe, a more faithful ecclesiology. I am asking, Does the very nature of the Christian community rule out the proliferation of Sunday services? And to that question I am more and more compelled to answer, Yes.

But let us suppose for the sake of argument that one accepts the principle of "one flock, one shepherd." Let us suppose further that the size of the congregation and the size of the church building are both optimum to support the "one flock, one shepherd" ideal. Even with these optimum conditions, other critical questions emerge. When shall we worship? And what kind of Sunday service should we "provide"? Traditional? Contemporary? Believer-oriented but also seeker-sensitive? Seeker-oriented but also believer-sensitive? With African American gospel music? With German chorales?

What will weekly worship look like in a "one flock, one shepherd" congregation? Well, like almost anything; there is almost always a multiplicity of possibilities when, prompted and inspired by God's Spirit, we attempt to construct something human. But whatever the shape and style and contour, worship in a "one flock, one shepherd" congregation will try to be faithful to two realities: the local, that is, the en-cultural; and the ecumenical, that is, the counter-cultural and trans-cultural.

Faithfulness to local realities will mean taking into account the actual geographical location of the parish. This is to note the necessity, in our worship as in all our discipleship, for the en-culturation of the gospel. For example, I am convinced that some kind of diocesan system is essential in contemporary church life, complete with geographic parish boundaries.

Faithfulness to ecumenical realities will mean, among other things, a commitment in our worship life to the unprecedented ecumenical consensus that has been achieved in recent years. This is a splendid gift of the Spirit in our day: an ecumenical consensus as to what Christian worship looks like. And it suggests the necessity for commitment, in our worship as in our ethics, to the counter-cultural and trans-cultural aspects of the gospel. It is a consensus visible in such documents as the *Constitution on the Liturgy* of the Second Vatican Council, and—more recently—the ecumenical document *Baptism, Eucharist, and Ministry* of the World Council of Churches.

What does this ecumenical consensus look like? Let me sketch eight characteristics of the ecumenical convergence in worship.

1. Christian worship is eucharistic. The chief service every Lord's Day will celebrate word and sacrament. More than that, word-and-sacrament worship will inform all other worship in the congregation and will thus train worshipers in sacramental piety.

2. The basic shape of word-and-sacrament worship is also part of the current ecumenical consensus. The service consists of two great actions. The first, the Service of the Word, is based on synagogue worship in Jesus' day, and includes hymns, prayer, and praise, with the reading of scripture and contemporary comment in the sermon on those readings. Intercessions and the exchange of the Peace flow into the second great action, the Service of the Meal, based on the ritual eating and drinking of the disciples with their Lord "on the night in which he was betrayed." There is consensus, further, that the meal itself possesses its own scriptural pattern: the bread and wine, like the life of Jesus, are taken into the embrace of God, blessed there, broken and poured out, and given for the life of the world.

3. Accompanying the one-room, radial, architectural plan in contemporary worship is the ecumenical preference for a free-standing altar, with the pastor presiding *versus populum*, facing the people. The chief architectural signs should stand out clearly: the font of baptism, the table-altar of the meal, the ambo for reading and preaching, the chair of the leaders' presidency. A bank of microphones with an electronic mixing board is simply no adequate substitute for these ancient, irreplaceable signs in Christian worship, no matter how familiar or contemporary such electronic gadgetry may be.

4. The worship environment will feature a one-room space, not a two-room space. Too many of our church buildings are still unmodified, axial, two-room spaces: the nave here, the chancel there. Such an architectural

arrangement for Christian worship is fundamentally flawed; it is not only hierarchical, it is monarchical, and thus inimical to the Reformation affirmation of the priesthood of all believers. Furthermore, in the leadership of this worship, laypeople will exercise their rightful roles.

5. A fifth conviction of the ecumenical consensus is the impulse to "enlarge the sign." This instinct—at least as old as Aquinas and Luther—attempts to correct what is perceived as an unfortunate human proclivity toward what might be called liturgical minimalism: "What's the least we need do for this to be a valid sacrament?" Partisans of the ecumenical consensus want to be certain that the sign stands forth always in fullness and clarity. Authenticity and fullness of sign: These qualities evoke the kind of "primary experience" for which modern North Americans are starved.

6. Still another conviction of the ecumenical consensus is a devotion to the rhythms of the church year calendar and to lectionary-based preaching.

7. A seventh conviction is that liturgy and ethics are inseparable. Peace and justice issues are squarely at the heart of eucharistic worship. The holy supper thus understood is celebrated as a true eschatological prolepsis, a breaking into the here-and-now of the future reality of the dominion of God.

8. A final conviction of the ecumenical consensus is that we are living today in a post-Constantinian age, more like the era of the primitive church (the "pre-Constantinian age") than like any intervening century. The church of the twenty-first century will have much in common with those earliest years of Christian beginnings: marginality and even persecution.

With the above commitments and constraints firmly in mind, we can begin to prepare the worship forms for a "one flock, one shepherd" congregation. As I have already suggested, we will want to preserve in some kind of creative tension the en-cultural, counter-cultural, and trans-cultural loyalties I have suggested above.

For example, if local (en-cultural) loyalties suggest the use of African American gospel songs as the primary musical voice in this place, then by all means, use them. But I'd want to insist that German chorales be given a place in such a setting on regular occasions, if for no other reason than to remind African American Christians of the catholicity of their faith (their counter-cultural and trans-cultural loyalties). And, of course, the reverse: European Americans need to hear and sing the music of their African American sisters and brothers for the same compelling reason.

Finally, what are the broad outlines, the contours, of what it might mean to be truly contemporary in worship? I would be willing to identify four aspects of the "modern" sensibility that subtly shapes our perceptions of the contemporary.

The first characteristic of the modern sensibility is *the evolution of abstraction* in all the arts. This modern sensibility has won for the visual arts in this century the same freedom of expression we have long allowed in music.

A second motif in the modern sensibility is the conviction that simplicity and restraint can often speak with more eloquence than wordiness and visual clutter. *Less is more*, the watchword of the Bauhaus architects, contains implications for preaching, worship music, prayers, and the environment of worship.

Still a third characteristic of the modern movement is the rejection of what might be called a Greek or idealized conception of beauty and an embrace of a Hebrew or functional conception of beauty. Again, the design principle of the International school of architecture has become the watchword of this impulse: *Form follows function.*

A fourth conviction of the modern era arises from media watchers: The medium is the message. Human beings communicate with each other in a rich variety of "voices": body language, gesture, facial expression, clothing, music, architectural space. We diminish a powerful voice—indeed, a chorus of important voices—when we remain ignorant of or insensitive to *the eloquence of nonverbal communication*, the media in which our message is cast.

This is an admittedly brief and simple overview of modern influences, the great cultural consensus of the twentieth century. For worship to be modern, one needs to look no further than the resources a worship book provides. There, the principles of simplicity, functional and/or abstract beauty, and nonverbal communication have been taken seriously.

Worship can be fully modern, fully contemporary, using only the fundamental pattern—the essentials of Christian worship—and the church's worship book. What is required of worship leaders and planners is simple, but difficult: judicious selection from among the riches—old and new—of the Christian tradition.

But the church—the worshiping assembly—offers the essentials and the riches to anyone who comes: to the older Christian and to the seeking soul. For that matter, there is a believer and a seeker in every human heart, in almost every given moment.

Together we need the one Word, the one bread and one cup, the one font of rebirth, the one Body, and the one Lord.

ABOUT THE AUTHOR

Paul Bosch is Lilly Visiting Professor of Religion at Berea College in Berea, Kentucky.

How can Christian worship be contemporary?

Marianne Sawicki

I remember the day my father died. He had not been ill, so the message to call home gave me no premonition. I phoned my mother, and she simply said, "Marianne, I have some sad news." She paused and sighed. "Daddy died today."

The feeling that I recall so sharply—one that preceded the flood of grief for myself, worry for my mother, questions about details—was the feeling that a door had swung shut. When Mama said "died," I seemed to see my father with his back to me, walking away from me, never to turn again and come close. We were no longer contemporary. This is death, as we know it: It shuts doors in time. On one side is the potential for intimate personal contact. On the other side the only contact is by memory, and memories gradually recede and fade.

When Jesus died, his friends had that same feeling of loss that we experience as bereavement. It makes no difference that he was going to rise from the dead. There must have been a time between his death and his resurrection when people grieved for Jesus. We can understand what his rising meant to them only if we look at it from the viewpoint of their grief. The loss of personal access to someone who has died is a "fact of time," that is, a basic structure of the way that human existence flows along. After Calvary, Jesus was seen by his friends as someone moving away—just as I saw my father in my heart on the day he died. But then, impossibly, Jesus was also seen as someone walking *toward* them and available to them in certain circumstances. Resurrection disrupts time as we know it.

We, today, are standing on the same side of Calvary where Jesus' friends stood, its futureward side: The side where, according to the laws of temporality, we can know nothing of Jesus except what comes down to us as memories. Even Jesus' contemporaries ceased to be "contemporary" with

22

him at Calvary. He became their past, and they became his future. Yet as the church, we are also saying (as did his friends) that we are in contact with Jesus—the Lord living in our midst—on certain occasions.

What kind of occasions would these be, then, that might make us contemporary with Jesus despite his death? Or is it even possible that such a thing could still happen among us? This way of framing the issue gives an ironic double meaning to the title of this chapter. "How can Christian worship be contemporary?" is either: (a) a practical question, promising a list of helpful hints to accomplish a goal that is desirable and do-able; or (b) a rhetorical question, suggesting that the phrase *contemporary worship* could very well turn out to be a contradiction in terms. In the first case, we would be facing the straightforward tactical challenge of remodeling our worship practices to keep pace with our times—a worthwhile goal. In the second case, we would be facing the much more subtle and strategic challenge of deploying Christian worship as resistance against the temporal distortions that wound humanity today.

Diagnosing temporality in our times

Among ritually observant Jewish men, there is a practice during prayer of binding the forehead and arms with bands containing words from the Law of Moses, as a sign to themselves of what it is that gives meaning and structure to their lives. We also bind our arms with a symbol of what sorts out and governs our existence. Our phylacteries are wristwatches. Although watches may seem to be tools for managing time, in a deeper sense they turn life into a resource that can be intricately controlled. For example, alarm clocks insure that the "temporal territory" before dawn is not a wasteland but is opened up and exploited; long-distance phone conversations are billed through an intricate system of timing and rate calculation. Time-keeping mechanisms regulate more and more of our lives in order to put them at the disposal of the economy for the activities of working and purchasing.

We have grown quite used to this, but it was not always so. The biblical stories of creation indicate that God created time—day and night and seasons—as a good thing and as a gift for human beings. Like some other creatures that we use, time is a blessing that has become bent out of shape. If the opening of a new territory for economic exploitation may be called "colonization," then our lives too are thoroughly colonized through the distortion of their temporal structure. The following are some examples of how contemporary westerners may experience time. These artificial cultural reconstructions of time are taken for granted and appear natural to us, but they are purposely contrived means of organizing our lives for the sake of marketplace interests.

Employment. We say of a job, "It's a living." (Really?) Having "work" means selling your time, perhaps eight or more hours a day. Those who are unemployed or underemployed may feel the burden of "time on their hands." The nonwork hours of the week also are organized around the needs of the job. Overtime work or professional conferences deplete the temporal resources available for relationships outside the workplace. The year is structured around vacations. A lifetime becomes a career, whose timetable may compete with the so-called biological clock of prospective motherhood or with the domestic needs of relatives at the extremes of the human time line: children and aged parents. One's skills gradually become obsolete, endangering one's job and livelihood. The temporal structure of work and career in our complex economy is designed to tap into life resources that could be allocated otherwise.

School. For children, school is much like work. It is an "investment in the future." Children must put aside some of the fun of childhood on the promise that their futures will be brighter for it. Young adults continue to spend long years in training for professions, on a time line that conflicts with childbearing and childrearing schedules. The most important lesson, taught covertly from kindergarten through graduate school, is that one must contribute one's time to the needs of the economic system.

Credit and finance. To borrow at interest is to become engaged in a peculiarly modern experience of time. The future is when you will finally own your home; but in the meantime you will have paid several times its value to the lender as interest. Actuarial tables define your life's possibilities. What we call "life insurance" doesn't protect life; it's just a bet between you and the underwriter that you'll die sooner than the odds predict. Time is the dimension along which real estate increases in value (for some of us), rents increase (for some of us), and money loses its value through inflation. The United States has a huge national debt that will have to be paid off by children yet unborn. It will be paid to the children of today's holders of bonds and T-bills.

Media and sports. Another kind of time experience takes over in front of the television set. Sports fans focus their attention on the dramatic artificial clock of the basketball or football game, perhaps as a way of diverting attention from events occurring in other temporal dimensions. Sports seasons and the evening's schedule of TV shows likewise are temporal anesthetics that can make us forget "what time it is" for the family. American history becomes entertainment in the docudrama and in myths like that of the taming of the Wild West. There's no clue that four hundred years of slavery and racial oppression underlie the commercials, sitcoms, and laugh tracks.

Fashion. Clothing, music, and cars are engineered to go out of style fast. They offer the illusion that a purchase can make you contemporary, that is, can keep you from seeming old and out-of-date. The quality of being "up-to-date" is a manufactured property, a cultural product that is made to appear desirable so that it can be sold. The same economic interests also determine that one narrow segment of the human lifespan is defined to be the most valuable and desirable. For men, this privileged time band lies between the ages of about 18 and 35; for women, it falls somewhat earlier and is much narrower. Little girls are sold the clothing that makes them appear older, at the expense of their childhood. Older adults are encouraged to buy the means of appearing younger. As part of the marketing of counterfeit youth, we are sold a view of our bodies as inexorably going "out of style." Time after a certain point (40? 30? 20?) is made to feel like it's going "downhill."

Ageism and old age. The people whom time pushes "over the hill" are culturally disparaged and sometimes economically disadvantaged as well. The passing of time for them means their increasing separation from the cultural ideal, as well as the real decrease of their self-esteem along with their physical powers. Any compensating gain in wisdom and experience, in family honor and love, is effectively camouflaged by what might be called the forces of colonization of time.

These are some of the distortions or "time warps" typical of our experiences of time.

Worship seems capable of affecting human time in several respects. On one hand, it can run with or run counter to the particular versions of temporal colonization that are characteristic of society. In doing this it can either wound or heal our humanity. On the other hand, worship can also disrupt time altogether by reversing the historical departure of Jesus and by identifying him personally with people who do not look like him.

Audiences and assemblies

In our well-intentioned efforts to "update" worship, there is a danger of inadvertently reinforcing some of the distortions catalogued above. In other words, tactical successes in making the liturgy *appear* more up-to-date can, in the long run, hamper its strategic ability to heal what has gone wrong with human time. Tactics like those mentioned below are not evil or stupid, and they have in some situations accomplished much that is worthwhile. Yet they merit reexamination as we ask what kind of temporality God wants for the kingdom and what kind of power we are given in the sacraments with which to fashion it.

Prayer as investment; investment as prayer. Jesus wrote the charter for capitalist Christianity when he told his disciples: "Store up for yourselves treasures in heaven, where neither moth nor rust consumes and where thieves do not break in and steal. For where your treasure is, there your heart will be also" (Matt. 6:20-21). This metaphor takes on a new and questionable meaning, however, when brought out of the ancient world and into the age of consumer capitalism. I have heard it preached that we earn time in heaven by serving time in the pew. I have heard it whispered that one secures a place in God's kingdom by contributing financially to the building of church edifices. It's hard to believe that Jesus meant to endorse no-pain-no-gain liturgy or "sacrificial giving" in those senses.

Audience shares and sound bites. The character of contemporary mass media is shaped by competition for the attention of consumers. In news reporting this pressure encourages quick and emotionally stimulating or even sensational stories about individuals at the expense of longer or more difficult analysis of conditions that affect the welfare of the whole society. The media shape us into impatient audiences unwilling to think hard about evil, where it comes from, and what can be done about it. They train us to choose breakfast cereals, but not to evaluate political claims that require understanding our past and planning our future. Conditioned as we are to be *audiences* of this sort, we find it terribly difficult to become instead an *assembly gathered for worship* on Sundays; perhaps we no longer can even tell the difference between an audience and an assembly. An audience hires the kind of preacher that it is accustomed to choose in the media: an anchorman, a talk show host, a comedian. Seminarians and newly ordained men and women feel keenly the conflict between their theological/ pastoral ideals and the tacit or expressed expectations of congregations (and sometimes of bishops) for sermons with good soundbites and for a crisply upbeat personal style.

Fashion and sports. While a gray-haired pastor may "look the part" for presidency of the Sunday assembly, the staff member charged with "youth ministry" has a different profile to fulfill. He or she should be younger than 30, play the guitar, and coach soccer. In other words, if teens and young adults seem disinterested in the church and its worship life, we may rush to the conclusion that the problem is one of style. A style problem can be fixed by applying a thin veneer of rock or folk music to make services more attractive to young people.

In this way of thinking, there are several hidden assumptions that need examination. (1) Should the worshiping assembly attempt to sell itself by mimicking fads engineered by the very market forces that are warping human temporality? (2) Isn't this tactic insulting to young people themselves and to the quality of their faith? (3) Can the service be "fixed" or "updated," if the real problem lies with the congregational misunderstanding of the time-structure of Resurrection faith?

Anesthetics and instant highs. The plague of drug abuse is commonly associated with the abuse of substances, but it may have even more to do with the abuse of temporality. Drug-induced euphoria is an instant gratification. It is sought in lieu of the warm glow of human intimacy, which would require too much time and patience to build. We are all "time abusers" because we have been conditioned to expect constant and intense gratification in our relationships, without spending time cultivating them and waiting for others and ourselves to grow into readiness for them. In worship we are impatient, too. By what criterion do we measure a "good experience" at liturgy: whether it has delivered a thrill and a chill, or whether it has nurtured the growth of the paradoxical peace that Jesus imparted on the evening of the most chaotic and disappointing day of his life (John 14:27)? One cannot tell right away how well the service has "worked." Designing the liturgy to produce instant rave reviews deflects attention from its longer-term consequences. This may even subvert them.

Nostalgia and antiques. What is the opposite of "contemporary worship"? Many would answer: "traditional worship." But is this an opposition that is helpful to pose? Surely there are senses in which all Christian worship must be traditional, and all Christian worship also must be contemporary. Perhaps "traditional" has become a code word meaning "the way we used to do things in my parents' church," or even, "the way I imagine things were done in the good old days"—whenever they may have been. An element of fantasy and wishful thinking lurks behind appeals to "tradition"—just as surely as advocacy of "the contemporary" masks complicity with some rather negative aspects of our culture's manipulation of human time and temporality.

Perhaps "traditionalists" and "updaters" can agree not to regard the Christian liturgy as a piece of antique furniture that needs refinishing so that it can stand prettily in a corner of modern life to remind us occasionally of who we used to be. Christianity is not nostalgia. Worship, in its forms and in its practice, is time therapy. It is the means for applying the power of the resurrection to heal the particular time-pathologies that give structure to western culture at the turn of our century.

The ends of time

The philosopher Martin Heidegger described human life as a way of "being toward death." I become myself in dying, at the conclusion of a life that has been nothing so much as a path toward that particular death. From this perspective, the event of my death will organize my life and give it its own definite character. Time, then, runs deathward, and each of us is on his or her own individual track. Heidegger saw that most people go to great lengths to keep from admitting this to themselves.

The desire to camouflage or deny death, the deathward trajectory of time, is what produces the pathological versions of temporality that were mentioned above: fashion, sports, media programming, investment, mortgages, credit, life insurance, and so forth. Even a secular philosopher like Heidegger would judge these to be inauthentic experiences of human existence insofar as they are geared to disguise the basic fact of our fragility and the inevitable loneliness of each death.

The Christian belief in resurrection has seemed to some critics to be just one more way to deny the reality and the seriousness of death, one more deliberate distortion of the structure of human time. In fact, this doctrine does announce the radical disruption of the futureward flow of human time, but it does so by facing death and taking it very seriously indeed. Jesus didn't avoid death; he defeated it. The resurrection came through Calvary, and what happened at Calvary remains the permanent basis for what happens at Easter.

To say that God has undone death in Jesus is to say that death no longer shuts the door and cuts off personal access to Jesus. In fact, the absence of Jesus through death is what makes it possible for Jesus to remain present with the church in the Spirit (John 16:7). Like everyone else who lived in the first century, Jesus is receding from us in time and his memory is fading. But alongside and through that historical withdrawal there is simultaneously an advance as the risen Lord comes toward us in our present and our future.

His eschatological advance toward us takes concrete form in various ways. We know what these ways are, because the risen Lord was already advancing toward his earliest followers after Calvary in those same ways, and the Gospel writers have told us what they are. The personal touch of the living Lord Jesus comes at us in the person of the poor and needy, in the Christian assembly at prayer, in the word of scripture and preaching, and in baptism and the holy supper. Worship makes us contemporary with Jesus and him with us. At least theoretically, that is what worship is for.

Is it unrealistic to expect that church services today should put Christians in position to be able to say with Mary Magdalene, "I have seen the Lord" (John 20:18)? Perhaps we need to replicate the conditions under which the Lord appeared to her (John 20:11-16). *First*, she was looking for him. *Second*, she felt the crushing reality of death and the loss of Calvary; she didn't deny it. *Third*, she went to the place where she had reason to expect that he could be found. *Fourth*, she persisted in her inquiry until she discovered him in the person of someone whom she had not at first recognized.

This gives us a pattern for what can and should be happening in the Christian assembly. A comparable liturgical recognition story occurs at John 1:26-39, situated at the place of baptizing. On the first day some inquirers are told, "Among you stands one whom you do not know." The next day Jesus is seen approaching and is identified by the Spirit and by John the Baptist. On the third day Jesus returns and invites two disciples to "come and see" where he is staying. Both of these stories have the same plot line: searching inquiry → Jesus found incognito → Jesus recognized → personal conversation → instructions for summoning or sending. The seeing of the Lord is something that happens in the midst of this process.

John's Gospel implies that the physical appearance of Jesus' body is such that he is not easily recognizable. (In other words, don't look for the familiar whiskers and the kindly smile.) Paul, too, alludes to the difficulty of "discerning the body" and the dangers of failing to do so (1 Cor. 11:23-29). The Epistles and Gospels were written to convey memories about Jesus from those who had known him before Calvary to those who wanted to know him afterward. But in addition to *memories*, these texts were written to convey *instructions* for recognizing the Lord in realtime, that is, for finding Jesus incognito in our present circumstances. Memories are easier to accept than instructions, because memories refer back to a past time; what they recall is presumed to be settled and closed. Thus it is relatively easy for us to worship eucharistically in the tradition of Paul and Luke, and to take up bread and cup *in remembrance* of the fact that Jesus lived here once upon a time (1 Cor. 11:23-26; Luke 22:19).

It is much less comfortable to seek Jesus in the present, even though we know where he is dwelling. It is difficult to worship *in expectation* of seeing the Lord in our lives. The possibility of hearing Jesus invite us into God's kingdom in the future depends upon responding to the invitations he gives us right now in the needs of the hungry, the thirsty, the homeless, the refugees (Matt. 25:31-40). Their pleas for help are coming from Jesus incognito. They are the only summons into the kingdom that we are going to get from Jesus. The future is now.

Christian liturgy is supposed to train us to recognize Jesus. The sacraments put us in a position to see and hear the Crucified One as someone living contemporarily with us. At worship we remember the past, but we also disrupt the temporal disconnection that "pastness" ordinarily entails. Christian worship is the end of time as we know it. In this lies its power to heal human temporality by resisting distortions of time like those suggested above as "colonizations" of human life by market forces.

A short list of how-to's

Worship "contemporizes" by bringing our time into the presence and power of the Lord Jesus, breaking the orderly continuity of history. Thus we mark life's transition points—births, marriages, deaths—with subversive reminders of their historical irrelevance, their anachronism. We assert that these points in the deathward flow of human lifetimes are also breakthrough moments into eschatological simultaneity in which the "past" of Jesus' death and the "future" of God's kingdom are happening "right now." We baptize into death; we bury unto life; we marry into relationships that are radically turned outward for the welcome and welfare of the community, not introverted into private pair-bonded self-sufficiency.

Liturgically, for example, the ceremony of confirmation and the character of the candidate's preparation for it are very different from other ritualized transitions that may occur about the same time—such as a driver's license test, the first paying job, or the junior prom. Baptizing a baby should feel different from a baby shower. The funeral liturgy discerns God's generous power at work in the life of the deceased, whereas the wake praises their accomplishments and regrets their loss. Weddings are perhaps the most difficult services in which to seek and meet the risen Lord; preparation for Christian marriage is easily overwhelmed by the details of planning the reception, the clothing, and the honeymoon trip.

Yet wedding feasts and garments were a favorite metaphor of Jesus in discussing God's kingdom. The construction of the invitation list was of particular concern to him. The "right kind of people" for a celebration of the presence of God's kingdom were the landless poor and lawless outcasts. These are the kind of people who in our society are victims of time, of distorted temporality. *Time victims* come in several varieties. Some are made homeless by the mortgage structure and the real estate market. Some are without health care because insurance companies disallow their "preexisting conditions." Some seniors are regarded as burdensome or unemployable just because of their age. Some parents must surrender their best hours to work at minimum wage, without time off when a child is ill.

When individual poor people need bread, it is relatively easy for us to respond. Time victims, however, are needy in other ways as well. Even those of us who have profited financially from the economic system that "colonizes" human lifetimes are personally diminished by it. For us it is much harder to allow God to disrupt the orderly relations of commodities and futures trading. The needed proliferation of loaves and fishes for the hungry seems un-doable to us, short of a miracle; yet we never doubt that an invisible hand multiplies wealth for the most deserving contenders in the marketplace. Have we become so satisfied with affirming real divine presence in the controllable commodities of bread and wine that we've lost our appetite for tasting the hunger of the Lord? (If so, snappier music isn't going to help.)

It's true that a church can boost attendance by reformatting the style of its services, just as a radio station can attract listeners by switching to a more contemporary broadcast format. But the ultimate effect may be to turn the house of God's people into a house of entertainment and sales. Sometimes people try to "fix" the liturgy before examining the health of the congregational life taken as a whole. But if the congregation decides that it truly wants to find the lordship of Jesus and is willing to let God disrupt the patterns of its days, weeks, and years, then worship can work.

ABOUT THE AUTHOR

Marianne Sawicki is Visiting Fellow of the Center for Philosophy of Religion, University of Notre Dame in Notre Dame, Indiana.

AFTERWORD

As you reflect on the proposals of these three authors, you might want to consider this: Each author's weighing of the open question of contemporaneity has itself been formed by the pattern found in the essentials of Christian worship. That is, *word and sacrament* do not only give us a *center* for our gathering. They do not only provide us with that thing of which we can ask, "Are we celebrating it in a way that is accessible to contemporary people?" They also give us a *method* to use in continually reaching toward such accessibility.

Paul Westermeyer knows that the pattern of Christian worship is always made up of at least two things. It is word and table, together. It is scripture readings (and then always more than just one) and preaching, together. It is thanksgiving and receiving food (and then both bread and cup), together. It is teaching and bath, together. It is leaders (at the best, more than one—both ordained and lay) and people, together. Christian worship uses these pairs because that is the only way it can faithfully speak the truth of Jesus Christ and so the truth of God. In fact, Christians believe that among these pairs *God is encountered in worship, not just talked about.*

Formed by this liturgical pattern, then, it is no surprise that Westermeyer finds that the music that serves a gathering in these pairs must also be characterized by at least two things. It must be old and new, local and universal, embodied and contemplative, powerful and broken. For the music of worship to be marked by only one of these characteristics is for it to risk losing its ability to serve. This is a theory of liturgical music that has been formed by the liturgy itself, and it is a theory with quite concrete practical applications. As you think about this proposal, can your own response, your own proposal, be similarly shaped by the deepest patterns of the center of worship?

Similarly, Paul Bosch has seen that the assembly for Christian worship is just that: an *assembly.* The church is not a collection of consuming individuals, choosing religious goods. It is a gathering of people who are, together, participating in the mystery of Christ and so being formed into one body. This principle is probably the deepest insight of the twentieth-century liturgical movement. But it is that very principle that leads Bosch to his striking proposal: *one flock, one shepherd.* Let there be one liturgy. More than that, he argues, is problematic for the very nature of the church and may say odd things about God.

All of these authors are concerned about the gospel being replaced by marketing. But Marianne Sawicki most powerfully identifies why such "marketing" may be among the ways in which we are hiding from death, wounded by time. Whether or not you agree with her analysis, you will be called by her back to the *method of the liturgy* itself: assembly for prayer, for word, and for sacraments as training to see the Lord *incognito* in the poor and needy, in the surprising places of our contemporary circumstances, coming toward us. Can you similarly be surprised by Christ's own contemporaneity? Will it be the contemporaneity of the resurrection of which we speak when we seek for our liturgies to be contemporary?

Gordon Lathrop

FOR FURTHER READING

Bosch, Paul F. *A Worship Workbench.* Chicago: Lutheran Council in the U.S.A., Dept. of Campus Ministry, 1971.

Collins, Dori Erwin. "Creating Relevant Worship." *Perspectives: The Changing Church* 11 (May 1994): 4.

Fleming, Austin. *Preparing for Liturgy: A Theology and Spirituality.* Washington, D.C.: Pastoral Press, 1985.

Hovda, Robert. *Indispensable Source: Reflections on Liturgy.* Ed. John F. Baldovin. Collegeville, Minnesota: The Liturgical Press, 1994.

Sawicki, Marianne. *Seeing the Lord: Resurrection and Early Christian Practice.* Minneapolis: Fortress Press, 1994.

Warren, Michael. *Communications and Cultural Analysis: A Religious View.* Westport, Connecticut: Bergin & Garvey, 1992.

Westermeyer, Paul. *The Church Musician.* San Francisco: Harper San Francisco, 1988.

Westermeyer, Paul. "Beyond 'alternative' and 'traditional' worship." *The Christian Century* 109, no. 10 (March 18–25, 1992): 300-302.